Persephone Heads for the Gate

The Gerald Cable Book Award Series

Love Fugue
Shulamith Wechter Caine

Blue to Fill the Empty Heaven
Joel Friederich

Dime Store Erotics
Ann Townsend

Best Western and Other Poems
Eric Gudas

Bodies that Hum
Beth Gylys

The Lessons
Joanne Diaz

Inventing Difficulty
Jessica Greenbaum

Close By
Gigi Marks

Why They Grow Wings
Nin Andrews

The Invented Child
Margaret MacKinnon

Odd Botany
Thorpe Moeckel

Bastard Heart
Raphael Dagold

A Parade of Hands
James Hoch

Winter Garden
Robert Hunter Jones

Lime
Audrey Bohanan

Where Is North
Alison Jarvis

Any Holy City
Mark Conway

Acacia Road
Aaron Brown

The Deepest Rooms
Randolph Thomas

Those Who Keep Arriving
Julie Danho

Sleeping Upside Down
Kate Lynn Hibbard

A Way of Looking
Jianqing Zheng

Natural History
Craig Beaven

Late Life
Stephen Ackerman

What Kills What Kills Us
Kurt S. Olsson

How News Travels
Judy Katz

The Odds of Being
Daneen Wardrop

Persephone Heads for the Gate

Merrill Oliver Douglas

Silverfish Review Press
Eugene, Oregon

Copyright © 2024 Silverfish Review Press

Library of Congress Control Number: 2024938676

ISBN: 978-1-878851-26-0

All Rights Reserved. Except by a reviewer, no part of this book may be reproduced or utilized in any form or by any means, electronic or mechanical, including photocopying and recording, without permission in writing from the publisher.

Published by Silverfish Review Press
PO Box 3541
Eugene, OR 97403
www.silverfishreviewpress.com

Member CLMP

Cover art: *Point* by Robbyn Zimmerman Tilleman. 2023. Mixed media. Used with permission of the artist.

98765432 First Printing

Printed in the United States of America

Contents

I.

SO MUCH 11
YOU GET USED TO IT 13
LIVING 14
SKELLY 16
GLASS 17
MARSHMALLOW 18
HALL CLOSET 19
SUMMER, IN MY EARLY TWENTIES 20
CROSSING THE LAWN WITH THE COMPOST BUCKET 21
HOME 22
FLIGHT 23
ON A GRASSY SPOT BY THE ROAD IN
    WARREN CENTER, PA. 24
PREPPING FOR THE COLONOSCOPY 25
MAY 2021: WE TAKE A BREATH 26
NO TRAINING WHEELS 27
"IMPROBABLE": 28
THE FUTURE 29
IT'S NOT LIKE I NEED IT ANYMORE 30
ALLIED MAINTENANCE 31
ANOTHER PAGE FROM THE GRATITUDE JOURNAL 32
THE CONFUSION OF TONGUES 33
HARVEST 34
BEYOND 35
THIRST 36

II.

WHERE I LIVE 41
BODY SONGS 47
AS IF WE COULD STEP THROUGH SOMEONE
    ELSE'S DREAM 51

III.

PERSEPHONE HEADS FOR THE GATE   57
ANOTHER POEM ABOUT MENSTRUATION   59
THE WOMEN WHO CAME BEFORE ME   60
ALL FLESH   61
HIGH   62
I TAKE UP YARN BOMBING   63
MY SELF   64
LULLABY   66
ROBIN WILLIAMS AT THE LAS VEGAS HILTON   67
THE DISTANCE FROM THERE TO HERE   68
GOING THERE   69
FONTAINEBLEAU   70
APARTMENT 3   71
BEREFT   72
WHILE OUR MOTHERS TALKED AND SMOKED   73
THAT MORNING   74
WHAT THE DREAM REVEALS ABOUT HER FATHER   75
MY MOTHER FRETS ABOUT THE SEATING CHART
    IN HEAVEN   76
END OF SUMMER   77
SEEKS ITS OWN LEVEL   78
EVEN HERE   79

Notes   81
Acknowledgments   82
About the Author / Cover Artist   83

For Ed Douglas, Jamie Douglas and Joan Emmer

And in memory of Lillian and Morton Oliver

I.

SO MUCH

When so much sun
      fills wall-sized windows,
            illuminates long hugs,
stories, sips of wine
      from plastic cups;
           when sun spills
kisses on men curled
      on park benches,
           softens the dream-stuffed
trash bags the men
      lay their heads on;
           when sun licks billows
of garlicky lamb smoke
      that roll above street fair earrings
           and rippling gauze blouses;
when daylight skips down
      scaffolding, taxis, flotillas
           of lake blue Citi Bikes,
lights up candy apple
      double decker tourist buses,
           streetside ticket hawkers;
when sun touches faces
      of cops ranged in line
           by the Garden, rifles slung
nose-down from belts;
      when late day sun winks
           at teen girls, phones tipped
precisely to line up cumulus puffs
      in the glass of One World Trade—
           girls born too late to glimpse
ghosts that forever pinwheel
      over that tower's shoulder;
           —when all that sun

rains down, I ride home
    drenched in such power,
        backbone, rib cage,
veins all buzz; it's impossible
    to say if this is pleasure
        or burn; I can't tell
if I'm drained or so swollen
    with voltage it might take
        hours to sing this light
back at the moon's face;
    I can't remember how
        to make legs lie still
under quilts as I listen
    for something called *sleep*
        to slide in like the D train.

YOU GET USED TO IT

The way you get used to the woman in uniform
rummaging your bag; the way you adjust
to roses with no scent, tomatoes like bloated
pool floats; the way it feels normal to stuff
desire in one pocket, compassion in the other;
the way you applaud smoggy sunsets and love
how fast your blood pumps when you snark
at jerks on Facebook; how cursing at robocalls
makes sense; how public shootings blur
with the more intimate asphyxiations; the way
you've stopped hearing the *chirp, chirp, chirp*
of the future in its wire cage—poor, fluffed thing
with its millet spray and a cuttlefish bone
to gnaw, how it can't stop plucking its feathers.

LIVING

1

Too much to do, short on sleep, I start making up
stories of how I'd die if I could choose:

head propped on pillows, linens starched and ironed,
comforters heaped on the bed, sun reflecting

off snow in the side yard, spilling through windows,
while down from the bedside radio floats that voice

like warm amaretto. He's reading poems,
bits of *Huck Finn*, the *Wall Street Journal*,

White Pages, what does it matter?
Eyes fall shut. Sleep trickles from cell to cell.

2

My father took five days to die,
head shaved and wrapped in gauze,

tube down his throat, machines pumping.
In the waiting room, I sat with maroon yarn

and needles I'd dug up somewhere.
Hour after hour. Each time a cousin or aunt

walked in, they asked, *What are you knitting?*
and each time someone cracked, *It's a chuppah!*

By the third day I'd given in: *Yep,
you got that right, I'm making a chuppah.*

3

This morning, R.—he's in his eighties,
taught me *Oedipus* and *Hamlet*, wasn't even

forty when I saw him last—writes, in an e-mail,
The cancer has moved to a place where there's no cure.

Now I'm sure it's time to dismantle the plastic
what-if Tinker Toy spools and sticks,

shake the Etch-a-Sketch back to its blank slate,
bang the door shut on the playroom,

surrender the corners to spiders, and start,
blight or not, on the job I was born for.

SKELLY

Everyone knew how to pack
crushed crayon stubs in bottle caps
and float those caps on hot water
to make the wax melt slowly.

Downstairs, we flicked them
from chalked square to square,
1 to 13, until someone turned
Killer and blasted the others away.

But first came the patient art:
playing the stove's flame
to trouble the water just short
of boiling, the soft crumbs

of Yellow and Scarlet,
or Aquamarine and Cobalt
undoing themselves
without pain, the way I'd like

to think the soul—
which I believe in only
when I hold my breath—
lets go at last, and then cools.

GLASS

A purple amphora
on fire with
liquid daylight

polished cube of
black that shoves away
all attempt to find meaning

jellyfish—
ribbony tentacles
lifted as though by sea swells

gilded boy
with curls blown back,
in the bow of a Baccarat vessel

knobbed green beakers,
African trade beads,
Tiffany windows,

pie plates, light bulbs,
bound sheaves
of optical fiber—

Leave the museum,
it's still everywhere:
blown snow bristling

with prisms,
splintered ice-platters
strewn on the river

all the world
breathing brilliance
inside this clear bell of cold.

MARSHMALLOW

Touch stick to fire:
        the flame I fish out
                blisters the surface black

like the Long Island *Press*
        pushed down the chute
                in those days when we incinerated

things we didn't need
        and sent delicate ash moths
                flitting over brick apartment towers.

So yes, when I bite in
        it flakes on my tongue
                with the taste of charred news.

But beneath that, sweetness
        that swallows the brain
                like when you hold your breath and

count, and count, and then can't.

HALL CLOSET

Slouched between the wall and seltzer crate,
I wound the crimped phone cord around
and off my hand and played with the empties'
cool, sloped shoulders: sapphire, emerald glass.
I liked how a press on the handle sucked a string
of carbon dioxide pearls up the tube, how the siphon
sighed, like the sound my grown body releases
now when I unfasten my bra. The cord
from the kitchenette stretched so far I could pull
the door shut through hours of talk with Vicki,
Fran or Louise. We all cracked the same joke:
my mother had walled me off from sex and drugs
with just seltzer for sustenance, safe with the rifle
my grandfather brought home from World War I.
It leaned in a corner, a danger to no one,
packed near the flare gun, helmet and mantis-
faced gas mask I might one day unwrap
from its canvas package and bind to my own face.

SUMMER, IN MY EARLY TWENTIES

Those weeks when the fan on the windowsill
mumbled apologies hour after hour,
I would wake up three or four times a night

and stand at the refrigerator
gulping cold water. Nobody told me
the taste on the mouth of the jar was just

rust from the lid: I was so sure
it was the kiss of disappointment.
Often, it was hard to tell the clutter

in my bedroom from the clutter in my brain,
loose stacks of magazines and notebooks,
postcards, paperbacks, all mixed up

with the name of some man who might
fly back from Costa Rica
or Nepal and hold still long enough to love me.

Nights when the t-shirt stuck to my back,
and I could feel the hairs sprout on my legs,
why didn't some grayer, fatter woman

sit me down and say, "Sweetie, this isn't your life.
This is weather." Maybe I did see the Empire
State Building's head on fire in a fog,

but by morning I would find it had cooled
to a blue coal, the streets all healed. Down the block,
the Italian ice guys would be lifting their garage door,

leading their carts out like ponies,
hosing them down, suds sliding in sheets
across the sidewalk and over the curb's lip.

CROSSING THE LAWN WITH THE COMPOST BUCKET

I might be a woman on a decorative plate:
a thumb-sized figure drawn in blue
on white porcelain, I daydream
my way over damp grass, the morning
a cool hand calming a brow.
The plate stands on a cupboard shelf
in the Antique Court of Shoppes, where
years from now, on a tour of Virginia,
I'll wander the aisles without purpose,
fingering Depression glass, trying on
fascinators, setting them back.
When I round a corner and spot
this dish, I'll halt mid-step and open
my mouth in a perplexed "O"—
as if I'd just found myself
walking behind myself, one impossibly
sunstruck morning in April
in my last life, or maybe the life before that.

HOME

That night when the plane droned in circles
over Indiana, waiting for permission to land,
the captain coming on every half-hour
or so to promise it would soon be our turn,
a child whining fitfully several rows back,
print in my book growing smaller by the minute,

that's what it feels like this afternoon: lead air
salted with colorless flakes lashed slantwise;
spruce trees muffled in dead weight, bewildered
limbs trembling; no plow, no mail, no news.

FLIGHT

The ten-year-old finds a wing suit
like the one she saw on TV,
but in her own size,
squirrel membranes fanned
from arm to hip. In her mind
she's zipped it on already
and gone gliding from roof to roof
in that spiked, glass-glittering city
she loves with a serenity
she'll never feel, when grown,
for husband, friend, or child.

In our first year, the man
I would one day marry
told me, given a chance
to help settle another world
—a one-way voyage, of course,
with no certainty he'd land alive—
he'd grab it, no question
or need to ask anyone's blessing.
And there I'd be, barefoot
in the dry grass, watering tomatoes,
watching the sun set and rise.

ON A GRASSY SPOT BY THE ROAD IN WARREN CENTER, PA.

      scatter of bricks
some crumbling, some still
        mortared in twos

or threes, stuck fast
      to what they were before—
disarray of leg bones

      one with its black hoof —
curved jaw, teeth
      intact, its shape a Norse ship

already sailed—
      fistful of vertebrae
throw the bones, what's next

                Don't be so mystical.
                      Brick or bone, it's just
           a rack where life hangs
                a while, then doesn't.

           Let weeds grow,
                or plow it all under
           and build a new house,
                set chairs on the porch.

PREPPING FOR THE COLONOSCOPY

Don't worry: this isn't the part you were expecting.

It's the part about the powder the instructions say to mix with four liters of lukewarm water and drink, one eight-ounce glass at a time.

That's seven glasses now, seven tomorrow morning. Vaguely citrus—concocted, I guess, to suggest lemonade.

But underneath, there's salt. And that viscous feel. No wonder when I tell myself, *Swallow*, my mouth doesn't know what that means.

The only way I'll get this done is with a straw at the back of the tongue, the smallest possible sips, so they roll without any willed action.

And still I need distractions. Sitcom. Magazine. I try counting sips, picturing the numbers like ice pops—purple, green, red, each glazed with frost—not checking what's left in the glass until I reach one hundred. Then start over.

This isn't hours of labor contractions, months of chemo, years in a cell.

There must be a way to accept each drop on the tongue like the single knowable fact in the world, the only life I get to live, neither vile nor delicious.

Think of that woman I saw yesterday jogging up the long, steep hill where I went walking. As she passed, I registered the slap of her shoe soles, each huff in and out. Was she counting, or just thinking, "…now…now…now…"?

The first glass takes ten minutes. I cross off the "1" in my notepad, unwrap a ginger candy, suck it to a sliver.

MAY 2021: WE TAKE A BREATH

At least for now we're still here, gripping
the end of the dog's stretched leash,
uncoiling a hose at the Scuffletown garden,
slowing from jog to walk while scraping
damp hair off the forehead, steering a stroller
with one hand, raising a takeout cup
to the mouth with the other, cloth mask
eased beneath chin like a new style
of sling or tentative extra smile, the tea
sweet and milky, child straining forward
over the safety belt, scanning shrubs
all down the block for a flash of tail or wing.

NO TRAINING WHEELS

Early Sunday, my father and I walk my bike to the courthouse.
He steadies the frame while I boost myself to the seat
and then he jogs, one hand on the back wheel's fender.
Squares of empty plaza slip beneath us, faster and faster.

Suddenly he's out front (*this is impossible!*) soft-shoeing
backwards, tongue loose, fingers wriggling near his ears like bugs.
I start to scream.

                But I know how this works:
all my life I've been watching that coyote in the cartoons.
Legs in a whirr, he shoots off the cliff and keeps wheeling straight
across a void that holds as long as he doesn't look down. So I don't.

"IMPROBABLE":

a lumpy mouthful, stuffed with rocks
and sofa cushions. Name for things I want:
improbable mounds of pistachio nuts,
improbable six months off from work.

The squirrel dangling head down, back
claws clamped to the feeder's perch,
belly stretched like a white sock
pinned to a line—is that improbable?

And when the squirrel curls straight up
to mouth more seed, with no more effort
than a bamboo shade, say what you like,
those abs are real. I saw them pull.

To stretch toward: Bridges, plazas. Improbable
keys in my pocket. Falcon wings. No GPS.

THE FUTURE

Like the mineral stain
you can't scrub from the sink,

like the knot of dark skin
on your pale thigh,

it doesn't declare itself.
Doesn't even arrive.

You just climb from bed
one Thursday wondering

how long since those seeds
of pain took root in your back,

or since some blend
of road salt and inattention

set loose the rust
that gnaws at your car

and at so many things
you still think of as new.

Now, home from the library,
look: bright spots of blood

on snow, up the driveway, the front steps.

IT'S NOT LIKE I NEED IT ANYMORE

Tissue from my uterus slipped free
and, touching an ovary, wrapped it—
so many sea star arms by now
they've melded. Try to unpick
this snarl, it could break, squirt cells.
No sign of cancer, but no test
is foolproof. Safest to pluck
the whole thing. But it's my call.

Dr. S., a little balder
than that day he caught my slippery
son and stitched me, lays out
how this works. The organ
will slide away clean as the white sack
I pull from a thawing roaster.
Liver, gizzard, heart—I eat just
the neck, give the rest to my husband.

ALLIED MAINTENANCE

When Ed worked third shift,
the best job was strolling the buildings
replacing dead lightbulbs.
Worst was the treater tower,
seven stories high, where lengths
of glass cloth, soaked in epoxy,
rolled past blasts of hot air. First
they pulled the blowers out:
then twenty or thirty guys
climbed the staircase that spiraled
the tower, and stood in the gaps. For hours
they scraped at gobs of dripped resin.

Sometimes the crew spent half the night
hiding. Ed napped in some engineer's chair
or made slow tours of the corridors,
ears alert for supervisors' boots, while Jeff Barr
cracked the day crew's combination locks, for fun.

If I'd been there, I'd have stuck
to my scrubbing, grousing the whole eight hours,
then gone home and switched off the lights,
aware I'd wake soon to the banging of trash cans,
or maybe to Ralph, the landlord's kid,
that basketball slapping a path
down the driveway, morning after morning.

On 2 a.m. lunch breaks the game wasn't poker
or blackjack, as I'd have guessed, but bridge.
Ed had the knack: he thought three moves ahead
and always knew which cards were still in play.

ANOTHER PAGE FROM THE GRATITUDE JOURNAL

Teasels: spiny, sculptural weeds,
their name a mix of muscle and seduction.

Squash vines that hop the fence
and race straight toward the woods.

Shattered pumpkins strewn across
a wet field, breathing, awaiting the cows.

Chicory and Queen Anne's lace
jitterbugging on the tongue of death.

Thorns, which keep me honest,
and poisonous mushrooms, silk-skinned.

THE CONFUSION OF TONGUES

At the tip of a pine
a bird I can't name,
whose markings I can't see,
unspools a multitextured rant
into the morning. Justice—
spurned love—hunger:
the notes disturbingly
familiar, dialect
impossible.

*

My neighbor's cap
says *NRA*, so I dislike him.
But he and his wife
sell honey and eggs, raise sheep.
The woman spins, dyes,
weaves. When I meet him
walking their tubby
brown dog, the man smiles,
wishes me a great day.

*

Those howls and yaps
that shock us from sleep,
surely they're the songs
of four ganged up on one,
hot fangs in soft fur.
But what if this is just
coyote doo-wop, young ones
braiding their longings
in harmonies closed to us?

HARVEST

The pepper plants
        Ed moved from the garden
                in white tubs, and hauled

indoors to live with
        the rest of our clutter,
                dropped all their leaves

by Thanksgiving. But now,
        with the ground hard,
                lawn still white,

they've slipped us flowers.
        One's even squeezed out
                a small fruit, gnarled

as a toothless gnome.
        We won't eat it.
                It's not food we're after,

just this off-kilter, out-of-
        proportion pleasure of seeing
                kinked, bare bones give birth.

BEYOND

Beyond the silver SUV whose driver,
    in clown makeup, grins and waves;
beyond two helmeted men
    on bicycles spinning downhill;
beyond the wind giving the pond
    on Ridge Road a rough back scratch;
beyond the cowboy cutout, slouched,
    one boot sole propped on a wall not there;
beyond the splayed squirrel, blood pooled
    in a wordless balloon by its head;
beyond my fingertip stroking the tail once,
    then snapping back to my pocket;
beyond and around and beneath it all
    there's this restlessness, thick in the air
as steam from cider, the whole world
    drenched, a seethe of insects flitting
and landing, rasping and dying.

THIRST

The aunt, in her hospital bed, takes two sips
of juice, then smacks the straw sideways, fingers
like twigs for kindling.

                    Coral lip gloss,
arrowed tilt of black liner at each eye, gone.
Hair spills like a small girl's over the pillow.

*

There must have been infinite water to waste
      in those years, bridges and fountains lit all night
like tiaras, ferries' backwash, ocean's ovation,
        high tide's fingers trailing up and down the beach.

Isn't she always the same age, impatient
      to sink her teeth in the next ripe plum,
keen to let go the rope swing and drop
      into any river, no matter how cold?

*

An old woman's breasts and hips
      are water.

An old woman's a young woman
      locked in a water-starved willow.

An old woman's a bundle of peeled sticks
      bound with tubes and pierced with needles.

The sum of her pills.

*

In a different country, long ago, women untied
their aprons, turned off the stoves, sent the kids

to the snack bar with fistfuls of change.
The women stretched by the hotel pool

whole afternoons in those years before God created cancer.
No one minded the peeled blue paint at the rim

or saw parched grass through the chain link fence.
They took long sips of menthol smoke.

Their red nails mirrored their lips.
Their cards were all aces, queens and kings.

II.

WHERE I LIVE

1.

Sometime during the night I find that the ground on which I live
has moved, reshaping itself so our house is now pinned to

the lip of a long slope, neighbors' homes small in the distance.
We used to look straight into trees from our windows.

Now we look down at them as if we'd been assigned
the cheap seats, top of the balcony: blue jays preening.

When I had this dream before, excavators gouged turf
by the mouthful, bulldozers muscled dirt into humps.

Workers in blaze vests talked into radios, unrolled blueprints.
But tonight it's all stealth and silence. No one asked us,

and we were so busy cooking dinner,
reading, we missed the disturbance. It feels

like that day I was driving our old but dependable
Ford, and next minute a wrecker was hauling the car

for scrap, my phone dead, cop shaking his head,
the tractor-trailer that had swiped me long gone across

the state line. Or it feels like when a diagnosis smacks
all sense of future from your hands, and you stand blinking

at your palm lines, bits of glass, small cuts, curled fingers.

2.

No one saw it coming.
The sky's mood turned,
rain thumped, river heaved

from its bed, a dripping firefighter
rapped the door, insisted
the neighborhood leave. They stuffed clothes

in a bag, grabbed laptop,
toothbrush, phones. The campus
field house filled with cots,

students passed out sandwiches
in cardboard clamshells.
Nights, the place smelled

of too many bodies, wet shoes,
snores rolled in and out, people
woke at all hours to soothe babies,

sit swapping rumors.
They knew what would happen:
at some point they'd go home

and find the river's paw marks
six feet high on the living room wall.
Then a week spent hauling water-

weighted couches, box springs,
rugs to the curb, soaked cartons
of stuff they'd been saving forever.

3.

I knew a man who once pedaled his bike across America.
Today he's some handfuls of ash in an urn. His collection

of books fills a wall in his nephew's childhood bedroom:
How to Succeed with Women. How to Make Money in Stocks.

I know a weekend market for collectibles that used to be
Game-It Family Fun Place, and years back, Philly Sales,

where I bought my son's shirts, cheap. It made sense,
he grew so fast. That store smelled of hot corn

and butter from the popper next to Costume Jewelry.
The floors were all scuffed wood. Nearby, the blank box

that used to be Kmart founders in its parking lot,
and here, the remains of Pat Mitchell's Ice Cream,

windows boarded, cone-shaped sign still topped in pink.
Across the street, what used to be Endicott Tire and Auto

until Ted's heart failed and his car hit a pole. Now
it's Discount Auto, its waiting room cleaner than Ted's,

no pizza crusts on grease-stained paper plates. The new guy
bought a point-of-sale machine that prints receipts. I miss Ted.

A woman I know lost the word for that dish she loved,
the one she cooked almost every week, like her mother

before her. She shapes it with her hands, squat oblong,
something with meat chopped up. She can almost catch it,

brown and warm, but it escapes, she rubs her tongue
across top lip, bottom lip, can't taste the name.

4.

Once more I feel my way
past iron-barred storefronts
and brick stoops. This dream

is a map I've checked and re-folded
so often it droops
in my hands, yet I remember

not a single street.
From where I lie asleep,
I see a blue bus

wheeze up a long hill,
headlights two white canes.
And at the end,

do I walk home? Or wait
by the Family Dollar Store
holding my transfer? I can't tell

Yonkers from Jamaica,
Korean from Spanish, I don't
remember when the El

came down, or if my skin
is the right or wrong color
for this neighborhood.

What made that park so small?
Whose headstone tilts there
turning black? Who sits

at the kitchen window
watching the sky catch fire
behind Manhattan,

husks of cracked
sunflower seeds
in a white plastic bowl?

5.

When you drag out the air mattress
blooming with roses of green-black mold;

when you strip back darkened cardboard flaps
and find holes in the bellies of plush bears,

birdseed and stuffing snagged in fur;
when you've bundled the mattress and toys

in trash bags and tugged those bags to the curb,
with the lamp from your father's workbench,

boxes of circuit boards, paperbacks stiff with damp;
once you've knocked down the thickest cobwebs,

smoothed and folded bubble wrap, taken a broom
to last year's leaves; once you've cleared enough space

to walk part of the way through the bottommost chamber
of your home's heart; once you've quit

coughing, gone up to shower off most
of the itch and grit, then maybe you can breathe.

6.

Lying for more than an hour
in the stutter of my husband's snores,
searchlights scouring the country

in my head, I try diverting
my mind onto the roads
I walk most mornings,

past the house of Myrna Senior,
past the driveway where Count
lived chained, past the garden

of pinwheels and glass baubles,
meth raid house, horse house,
woods a man called Bob

bought and thinned to park
his new camper. I hope that
by the time I reach the house

where moss has overwhelmed
the roof, I'll have crossed without
knowing onto the dream road,

the way I might cross
from Eastern to Atlantic Time
to Newfoundland, always a half-

hour out of step, and find myself
smiling on the summit of that dream
hill, elbows on warm stone,

field glasses scanning the ocean.

BODY SONGS

Age 6

Under the blankets
further adventures: tonight
I'm the beautiful
mouse girl the alley cat
kidnaps and forces to
sing and dance for his pals
in the saloon.
(I must have cribbed this plot
from Farmer Brown cartoons.)

One night he takes me
to the hospital
to get an operation
that will make me so badly
want to marry him
everyone will see the heart-shaped
thump! thump! thump!
through the lace of my gown.

Age 11

My friend and I ride
Jamaica Transit to Far Rockaway
to see the movie "Help!"

Bright sun, a beach in the Bahamas.
Paul McCartney in a snug black t-shirt
holds a girl wearing a bikini
the way he would hold a guitar. Strums her.

Age 15

The boy I like
skates the tips of
his fingers down
the nape of my neck.
Among these kids
on the benches,
I'm a singing bowl.
The long note
spreads to the tips
of my breasts.
No one has ever
felt this.

Age 24

sleeveless, barefoot,
      this iced drink
the first straight whiskey
      of my life and the
longer I dance
      the wider my mouth
the hotter my face
      the faster my caution

spatters off the ends
      of my hair
           into the palmettos

Age 26

I slide
beneath the quilt

and again
my single bed

is a funeral
boat, in which

each night
the tide drags

my still form
back from this

golden knot
of cafés, homes,

streets, back over
tilting,

flickerless stretches
of cold.

Age 33

The day I feel
the baby quicken—
skitter of bubbles,
moth wings on glass—

first thought:
I've been cheated—
something inside me
not me

second thought:
I've become
      the split seed
           of a bean plant
                aloft on the
                      bean sprout's tip
                            as it uncurls
                                  into daylight.

AS IF WE COULD STEP THROUGH
SOMEONE ELSE'S DREAM

Such a long time I stand
in my driveway watching
smoke from the neighbors' wood stove
roll straight up. In the frame of his window,
Joe lifts a coffee can from the top
of the refrigerator, sets it on the table.

What would he think if he saw me drop
him, red plaid bathrobe and all,
in this poem? I put people in poems
all the time but can't picture myself
a quick blue sketch
in another person's morning,
small woman toiling up Underwood Road,
scarf wound across her face.

*

That apron—
lit from behind in a ground floor window,
young woman bends to set a plate,
maybe a roast or pie, on a table.
It thrills me, that gesture seen, lost.
April twilight, eighth grade field trip,
somewhere on the road between Gettysburg
and Lancaster, face to chilled glass.

Where I come from, we live in rows
piled onto rows, walls
of red brick filled with windows,
each with a story I have to invent:
three frozen dinners warm in the oven,
TV flickers, a girl with a stuffed nose
winds her hair on pink rollers.

*

Out of the Metro, across the Mall,
up steps to the National Gallery,
through the grand hall, more stairs,
then a slow perusal—three rooms,
four or five centuries. We stand
a long time at one framed page:
Little Nemo in Slumberland.
Nemo and the Princess climb
the spiral stair of the North Pole—
as if we could step through
someone else's dream,
move up by reading down
and across the stacked squares.

As soon as they reach the top
the pair has to retreat—
one thousand slippery steps—
to beat the storm that spews
on the hour from elbowed pipes.
The bottom panels fill with snow,
a pattern like antique wallpaper
seen through a window.

Three days later, the Gallery's closed,
government shut, the Mall dozes,
bewildered tourists drift
from museum to museum
in search of the smallest crack
to let them slip through just one door.

*

At Price Rite, a man and woman,
each with a shopping cart,
stand in the pasta aisle talking
for such a long time
I have to walk a different way
to reach the Parmesan.

They sound like former neighbors
catching up, first chance
in ages, filled carts standing
nose to nose, quietly grazing.

The cashier named Alice calls:
I can take you on Ten. A gray-brown
braid lies thick on the back of her blouse.
By the exit, two boys
stand on tiptoe, faces mashed
to the sides of the claw machine.
Is it the mountain of stuffed toys
they dream of? Or do they love
the shapes their squashed lips make,
prints they leave with breath?

In the parking lot, my trunk lid strains
against ice. I have to tug and tug
to crack the trunk open.

*

Ice and glass and sun and colored
lights on strings, days of the week
like glass beads
on an abacus, wind bats
traffic lights back and forth
above cars as the sky grays.
Home, the kitchen light grows warm
with the smell of meat in the oven.

Propped in the window, a daisy
of stained glass my roommate's
boyfriend made half my life ago.
They broke it off, and Mary left
this flower behind when she moved
to the city. Eric went back to Ohio.
I've lost touch with Mary, too.
That square of glass is junk, but somehow
I can't throw it out or give it away.

III.

PERSEPHONE HEADS FOR THE GATE

The lines in Hell move faster.
But here, the not-yet-departed

drop their shoes in trays, shrug
bags onto the belt with the serenity

of people who believe that what the
tunnel swallows always comes back.

Even travelers whose flights are delayed
indefinitely know where they're going.

I, though, can't read the print
on my boarding pass. No matter:

any landing is sweeter than millennia
spent shuttling—winter, summer, winter.

On one side, my husband, who climbs on top
each night, then snores in my ear.

By day we slouch on our twin thrones
while shades of the dead flick past.

On the other side, Mother, table piled
with olives, figs, those loaves she wakes

before dawn to knead. If I don't eat all
she'd like, she spoon-feeds me custard.

Evenings, we sit in her bed and watch
Jeopardy, two stone goddesses

blurting out all the wrong questions.
In Terminal C, though, I am no Daughter

or Queen, no half of a whole,
no reason for fat wheat sheaves

or glazed fields of stubble. Here
I am just this person,

pockets stuffed with tissues,
who slides her right foot, then her left,

into thin-strapped sandals, fastens the buckles.

ANOTHER POEM ABOUT MENSTRUATION

We were the moon's sworn sisters:
rhythmic, sticky, glistening.

That was an article of faith.
But now I'd swear, if any goddess

took me in charge back then,
she was not the moon: she was

a squat, dripping creature
with foul breath dragging her bulk

across the living room, clutching
a nightstick to jab in my back. Call her

goddess of stained jeans soaking
in the bathroom, of super-absorbent

overnight pads, name her shambling
mud-nymph of clots, of tampons

like dead mice, mother of headaches
that drowned out the newscast,

of days when I slunk from desk
to toilet, days when I had to lie down,

who left me to leak in the blankets,
who trilled her alarm in my bones.

THE WOMEN WHO CAME BEFORE ME

They buttoned their thick tweed coats to the chin
and nagged their kids to tug knit hats low on their ears until April.
They knew the price, to the cent, of canned peas at each of three
    markets.
On Sundays they'd sit face to face in the kitchen, slapping down
    coupons
like aces and jacks, swapping stories about Manya and Sonya
and Selma, and Abe from downstairs. They boiled the orange out of
    carrots,
tucked a cooked egg in the meatloaf, swore by Tab and Melba Toast.
They scrubbed the linoleum spotless but never walked if they could
    catch a ride,
never got wet without bathing caps, never went barefoot.
All these years I've been trying to outgrow those dresses they
    shortened
to fit me, working on their knees, mouths bristling with straight
    pins.

ALL FLESH

Dressed in bristles, they look naked,
rooting in earth in plain sight with wet,
flexible snouts. Such intimate parts
to probe the world. They've stripped the leaves
off weeds and ploughed the stalks down,
scissoring roots like silk curtains.

Nothing is hidden. Grubs, slops, apples—
all they devour turns to ham
in time, sweet sausage, chops wrapped
in white butcher paper. Yet they smile.
They trot to the barbed wire, grunting
and blowing to sniff at an outstretched finger.

Truly, on mornings like these it's delicious
to immerse your face in mud and then arise
all round and glowing like a woman at a spa
who loves soft cheese and dark chocolate
and adores those wedge-heeled pumps that
so slyly show off the shape of an ankle.

HIGH

I'm not much of a drinker,
but isn't it fine
how a sip of whiskey
can fix its hooks under my arms
and hoist me an inch or two
above the kitchen vinyl?

I love how I stay there,
still myself, but taller,
drifting from fridge to sink
to stove as if wearing
a flashier woman's
spike-heeled slingbacks.

And what a relief,
since my fingers have lost
all touch with my brain,
that there's no blood spilled
on the leeks, and the rice
pot hasn't boiled over.

I TAKE UP YARN BOMBING

Because it's so difficult to love November's
ashes, streaked mud, cobwebs, husks.

Because I remember small brown birds
going *chink, chink* like coins in the ivy all winter.

Because the kid with all the oil pastels
grew up and moved someplace warmer.

Because even after twenty-five years,
I regret letting go of that peacock mask.

Because nostalgia is a perilous elixir—
addictive, it makes the throat go numb.

Because the way to kill that desire
is to cap the bottle, swallow the spoon.

Because some women have the power
to turn parking meters into mermaids.

Because graffiti is the city's icy river:
drink it, or dive in and swim.

Because the road doesn't run forever,
but quick feet throw off rainbows.

Because what I need right now is
a thick, fruity syrup to pour on my fear.

MY SELF

There were two of me,
not twins, but two
halves of one self
in two distinct bodies.
Nothing strange in that

by the math of dreams.
But in this dream
one me had died
the previous night—
disease like flash flood.

So why did the me on the bus
that day feel nothing
missing? I stepped off,
climbed to the overpass,
paused as usual to pick

from black, fat mulberry
clumps that drooped
by the guard rail. Then,
at my parents' house,
through the red front door,

my mother's voice
keening the loss
of her of firstborn.
Wouldn't she be glad
when I walked in?

*

Today, the me who reads
the words of the me
who wrote down the dream
thinks, *Look how neat
that girl's cursive;*

the me who holds
the old notebook crushes
berries in her teeth
in memory, feels the rain
shiver off leaves;

the me who walks
here now, who sees
how the world took shape
in the eyes of the me
who took notes—

how many are we?
Arm-in-arm,
a chain of newsprint
cutouts posed between
face-to-face mirrors,

see us stutter
endlessly backward,
forward, time gone,
time to come,
smaller and smaller.

LULLABY

My mother swears by a relentless
jiggling she says bores infants to sleep,
but you're so furious, nothing stops you

who've never heard of first shift
or your father's alarm. At night
when I slip in to undress

I hear him twisting,
twisting in the damp sheets.
You're hardly his son now,
just a loud neighbor. The radio's

seething, I lift you, we're sticky
and slick as I stamp from couch
to table to couch. You're red
as this morning's sunrise, and tomorrow's.

My palm cups your head, we're both crying,
I'm jumping in place, hissing Stop please
please stop it! And bouncing higher
and landing so hard the lamps rattle.

ROBIN WILLIAMS AT THE LAS VEGAS HILTON

Dead Elvis and dead Marilyn, no shock to spot them
strolling the exhibit hall, arms linked, flashcube smiles, striking
pose after pose by a tower of Goodyear tires.

You were alive then. Still, a Gold Sponsor could hire a man
to be you for one hour: Hawaiian shirt dipping like wings
among dark suits, straight skirts, sushi, cheese puffs.

Truth: I nearly dropped my wine and fled.
Because I loved you. Nose, cheeks, laugh lines—as private
as if I'd designed them. Your vowels in my pulse,

tape deck spinning *Aladdin, The Fool
and the Flying Ship*, late afternoons in the car,
my son in his child seat softening into his own hum.

In Vegas that evening, the man who was not
you clasped my hand in both his hands. I blushed
like salmon flesh laid bare on a bed of white rice.

THE DISTANCE FROM THERE TO HERE

A kayak is no more than a skin
worn to sit on water.

Seneca Lake is forty miles long
and my son is a bean in a thin pod.

The wind blows the wrong way:
the broad surface darkens.

I brace my feet and haul
hard on the paddle with cold hands.

The boy is a thistle seed
and the lake's iron mouth pulls wide.

Waves shove me north.

GOING THERE

I visit the campus
web cam once or twice daily.
I won't see my son: I just want to check
on the air he inhales, sneak
a look at snow or sun whitening the paths
in that place where he walks.

*

Google sets me down on Herzl Street,
exactly the spot where I see my dad lifting
this toddler who grew to be me. A slight screen-
twist brings up the same brick, two-story
houses that rise at our backs in the photo,
as if I could step through glass
into black-and-white Brooklyn
and nuzzle that young man—thirty-five or so
that day, just a few years more than the girl
will have lived when the stroke knocks him dead.

*

Those videos the terrorists post—
no sane mother would watch.
But at night, awake on her back,
she hears blank screens taunt
from all over the house:
*Switch on the power. You need
to feel blade touch neck.*

FONTAINEBLEAU

I say she stole it.

How else would a silverplate
teaspoon, stamped with the crest
of a world-famous five-star hotel,

turn up in the box
of plain flatware my grandmother
left in our crawl space?

She took a small apartment
in Miami Beach each winter,
for years. So it makes sense:

maybe she went to some banquet, Hadassah
or National Council, with prime rib
and green beans, a congressman giving the keynote.

She'd have worn a knit pants suit,
and diamond earrings
and sat with her best friend, Gussie.

And maybe towards nine, while her decaf
with non-dairy creamer grew cold,
and the chairwoman wrapped up her thank-yous,

what if the union seamstress who still drove
the needle through thick wool coats
some nights in my grandmother's gut

hissed something sharp and short,
and what if she stretched her palm
to smooth the cloth by her plate,

and the first cool, lustrous thing it touched
fell into her handbag along with the usual
couple of packets of Sweet n' Low?

APARTMENT 3

They shared a room
so narrow that from twin beds
pushed to opposite walls,

a girl could reach into
her sister's dream and take
what she needed:

once
    a dollar
once
    a lipstick
once
    a furred animal

drained of its life
to drape on the collar
of a black cloth coat,

glass eyes glued
in arrow-shaped head,
tail caught in a steel clip
where teeth would have been.

BEREFT

I lost the silver pendant
Malka gave me when I was eight.
Lost my grandmother's spoon
and great-grandfather's teapot
and cracked Jane's Japanese cup.

I lost Jon Cohen entirely—
eighth grade teacher,
sideburns, blue eyes, name
so common Google shrugs.

Mrs. B's print cotton robe,
a Christmas gift, I cut for dust cloths.
Ann's peasant blouse I've worn
down to patches and threads.
Now Ann's gone.

Monkees albums, guide to the World's Fair—
vanished. Also the ten or so chords
I learned on guitar.

I drop more Yiddish year by year,
and I must have misplaced my father,
my cat, the white dress,
the infant I nursed, the sticky toddler.

How many years till a swollen river
swallows the shoebox of mail,
the photos, cassette tapes, thumb drives,

and leaches the ink
from my twenty-six journals,
every loop and dot of this life
sipped off like so much vodka?

WHILE OUR MOTHERS TALKED AND SMOKED

In the bushes near the iron fence
we'd sometimes find a bottle,
contents drained, but around the lip
a brown crust of sharp-scented sugar
we'd pick off and sniff on our fingers.

I knew those bottles came from men
called bums, whom I'd spot here and there
on the benches, turned around
the wrong way, knees wedged
into the space between seat and back rest.

No one's neighbors, no one's uncles,
they lay their foreheads on crossed arms,
bellies lifting and falling,
as fiercely asleep as our brothers
and sisters tipped back in their strollers,

plastic nipples loosed from the babies'
slack mouths trailing glints of milk.

THAT MORNING

After nurses untangle the wires from his
      body, each of us takes a turn to
cross the floor and touch him: Daughter.
      Daughter. Wife. So loud, this absence of
exhale and inhale. Egg-smooth curve of
      forehead and shaved scalp innocent of all
gauze now, no IV drip, no ribbed tubes.
      His ringless hands have swelled, still warm.
In minutes, their own hands chilled,
      jaws sore, several women
knitted in history and blood
      load into the Plymouth and head for
my mother's kitchen where, coats dropped,
      no one thinks to ask what's next.
One aunt slices tomatoes,
      pulls at a head of romaine; her sister
quickly opens cans, then
      reaches across the counter to
scrape white tuna chunks into the
      turquoise bowl my mother has been
using forever, while my mother stands
      vacantly blending in Miracle
Whip with her red-handled chopper,
      Xs rocking over wobbled Xs. We have
yet to pick up the phone, not ready for
      zero hour, kisses, the threshold.

WHAT THE DREAM REVEALS ABOUT HER FATHER

1

The funeral? It was a hoax.
He's lived for years in this walkup,

dishes washed,
shelves stacked with soup cans.

There's no young wife, no collection
of semi-skilled, half-finished paintings,

just this day bed, a TV.
Each morning he chooses a clean shirt,

takes the "F" downtown,
works, rides back.

2

He stands at the window,
forehead to glass

such a long time,
maybe he's dozed off.

But just as I start
toward the door, he turns:

Listen. I'm fine.
They give plenty of heat.

No leaks. No roaches.
And where did you ever

see walls this thick?
(He knocks.) *I swear*

I haven't heard another
human voice in years.

MY MOTHER FRETS ABOUT THE SEATING CHART IN HEAVEN

*What if they place me with my parents,
not my husband?*
Then she'll be stuck for eternity

cutting the veal on her plate
into smaller and smaller pieces,
listening to my grandfather

puffing his cheeks,
my grandmother coaxing
the angel-faced waiters,

so sleek in their long curls
and silvery jackets,
to bring her a bigger lobster.

Miles across the hall, my dad's
been paired with his best friend,
Marty. And off to the side

sits Marty's wife,
Roslyn of the tiny waist,
wisp of a smile on her pink mouth,

smoke uncurling from the Newport
tipped between her fingers.
Look at them: Marty

and Dad, slurping egg creams,
reliving whole Dodgers games,
scatting "Take the A Train."

END OF SUMMER

It's an old game I play
with my niece's toddler,
on patchy grass
behind Bill's Kitchen.

We're giving his parents
some time alone
with their burgers and fries.
The grass is thick with rocks.

We take turns choosing—
cracked disks, rounded wedges—
fitting them belly to hip
on my takeout container.

Quickly, the flat white
surface fills with decisions,
the kind you can take back:
flip the box, start over.

Child and woman
sorting the earth's bones
under a sky like a lens
the sun squints through.

SEEKS ITS OWN LEVEL

1.
In the city, a child fills a shovel with snow from a ridge the plow made, then stands between parked cars and dips the blade in the flowing gutter. The snow bleeds clear in water that tangles toward the storm drain, dragging filter tips and ripped leaves. That drain is a horror, its stretched mouth. Surely it's too narrow to take her, but aren't there places you can't see coming where the rules don't apply and then you're gone?

2.
The boys fill plastic buckets from the spigot near the bathrooms and stiff-leg it back to the playground, built on sand. They pour the contents into the hole they dug beneath the slide and run back for refills, over and over. An entire swimming pool at their disposal, but they love this best, water they can master, earth that swallows only so much before the water settles in to make a pond.

3.
Some summers it never rains. The river shrinks, skeleton protruding. They let the child's bathwater stand overnight and, in the morning, carry it in soup pots to pour on the peppers and tomatoes. Some years it rains so much the river is a foaming brown pestilence among trees. Storm sewers back up into rec rooms. The lawnmower's wheels cut black spirals, a hieroglyphic curse when seen from a low-flying plane.

4.
By June, the creek behind the house is barely deep enough to wet her feet. The ooze at the bottom feels the way cool juice tastes. It's a blessing she never asked for, jagged comma, pause in the downward slope, visible on no map, a crease in the succession of years, banks thick with violets and touch-me-nots, star moss, two-inch seedlings that yearn toward the branches that dropped them.

EVEN HERE

> "I think I could stop here myself and do miracles."
> —Walt Whitman, "Song of the Open Road"

Even here, among wrapped bricks
of muenster and cheddar,
as I step past a wall of blue
soup cans, that altar
to the salt-infused consolations,
walk past foam trays crowded
with drumsticks and pork chops,
past tubs of non-dairy topping, even
here I could pinch together
thumb and index finger to tweeze
unending filaments of joy from the air,
one strand of ribbon
candy following another, watermelon
tangerine, mint. Even now
as I swing the stuffed cloth bags
from counter to cart, and young Tanya
hands me a receipt so long
I wind it around and around
my thumb to fit my wallet,
and now when I halt my cart
beside tiers of iced cupcakes and
transparent clamshells of croissants
to drop wallet in backpack,
rezip, set strap on shoulder
and roll toward a Sunday the color
of batting revealed through
the rents in an old comforter,
couldn't I stop here and do miracles
until those electric doors
fling wide their arms to receive me?

Notes

"Skelly": Skelly is an urban game played on the sidewalk, using weighted bottle caps. Also called skully, skelsies and other names.

"Hall Closet": In my New York City childhood, the seltzer man delivered wooden crates of seltzer water in bottles with built-in siphons—the kind of bottles the Three Stooges and others comedians in old movies used to engage in seltzer battles.

"Where I Live": Newfoundland—part of the Canadian province of Newfoundland and Labrador—has its own time zone, which is half an hour ahead of Atlantic Time. When it's noon in Nova Scotia or New Brunswick, it's 12:30 p.m. in St. John's, NL.

"Another Poem about Menstruation": This poem was inspired by "poem in praise of menstruation" by Lucille Clifton.

Acknowledgments

Many thanks to the publications that previously published some of the poems in this book, sometimes in slightly different form:

Abandoned Mine, "Beyond"
A Narrow Fellow, "Lullaby," "While Our Mothers Talked and Smoked"
Baltimore Review, "Seeks Its Own Level," "Summer, in My Early Twenties"
Barrow Street, "All Flesh"
Briar Cliff Review, "Even Here"
Cimarron Review, "The Women Who Came before Me"
Connotation Press, "Fontainebleau"
Crab Creek Review, "Allied Maintenance"
Cumberland River Review, "Marshmallow"
Eunoia Review, Section 5 of "Where I Live," "What the Dream Reveals about Her Father"
Journal of Compressed Creative Arts, "Apartment 3"
New York Quarterly Magazine, "Another Poem about Menstruation," "It's Not Like I Need It Anymore"
San Pedro River Review, "The Distance from There to Here"
South 85 Journal, "Bereft," "Crossing the Lawn with the Compost Bucket"
Stone Canoe, "Glass"
Sugar House Review, "Flight," "Harvest"
Tar River Poetry, "Another Page from the Gratitude Journal"
Valparaiso Poetry Review, "Home"
Whale Road Review, "That Morning"

In addition, some of the poems in this collection were included in the chapbook *Parking Meters into Mermaids*, published in 2020 by Finishing Line Press.

Thank you to Rodger Moody for choosing *Persephone Heads for the Gate* for the 2022 Gerald Cable Book Award, and for so carefully helping this book through publication and into the world.

Deep gratitude to the Grapevine Poets, friends who have been meeting for years to share our work, offer suggestions, talk shop and provide mutual support. In many ways, you make my life as a poet possible.

About the Author

Merrill Oliver Douglas's poetry chapbook, *Parking Meters into Mermaids*, was published in 2020 by Finishing Line Press. Her work has appeared in *Baltimore Review*, *Barrow Street*, *Tar River Poetry*, *Stone Canoe*, *Little Patuxent Review* and *Whale Road Review*, among others. Raised in New York City, she holds a B.A. from Sarah Lawrence College and an M.A. in English from Binghamton University. She has worked as an arts administrator and business journalist, and since 2000 she has run a freelance writing business from her home, near Binghamton, NY, although she is currently edging toward retirement. Merrill participates in a local poetry workshop called the Grapevine Poets, and since 2022 she has been part of the Boiler House Poets Collective, which does a residency each fall at the Studios at MASS MoCA in North Adams, MA.

About the Cover Artist

Robbyn Zimmerman Tilleman first began making art at age two, when she would sneak a pencil into her bedroom at bedtime so she could draw on the sheets. She was admitted to the High School of Music and Art in New York City and then continued her creative education informally while getting degrees in social work. Upon retirement, she has embraced her passion for creating art and has won awards and accolades in many juried shows, including a blue ribbon in a statewide art competition for her mixed media painting. One of her pieces was chosen to appear in a Lifetime movie. Her work is currently on display at The Artisan Village Gallery in Eatonton, GA. Robbyn lives with her husband Joe and dogs Pippa and Biscuit in Milledgeville, Georgia. Instagram: tillemanart

The interior text and display type were set in Adobe Jenson, a faithful electronic version of the 1470 roman face of Nicolas Jenson. Jenson was a Frenchman employed as the mintmaster at Tours. Legend has it that he was sent to Mainz in 1458 by Charles VII to learn the new art of printing in the shop of Gutenberg, and import it to France. But he never returned, appearing in Venice in 1468; there his first roman types appeared, in his edition of Eusebius. He moved to Rome at the invitation of Pope Sixtus IV, where he died in 1480.

Type historian Daniel Berkeley Updike praises the Jenson Roman for "its readability, its mellowness of form, and the evenness of color in mass." Updike concludes, "Jenson's roman types have been the accepted models for roman letters ever since he made them, and, repeatedly copied in our own day, have never been equalled."

Front cover title, author name, and all back cover text were set in Garamond. The sans serif text at the bottom of the front cover is Helvetica Neue.

> Cover design by Martina Salisbury, TWOSEVEN INC.
> Text design by Rodger Moody and Connie Kudura, ProtoType
> Printed on acid-free papers and bound by Bookmobile